CHERISH THE BONE

To Tom Woodman —

Your encouragement and belief in my work helped me bring my poems to fruition. Thank you.

Sheila Burke

CHERISH THE BONE

Poems

Sheila Burke

iUniverse, Inc.
New York Lincoln Shanghai

CHERISH THE BONE
POEMS

iUniverse books may be ordered through booksellers or by contacting:

iUniverse
2021 Pine Lake Road, Suite 100
Lincoln, NE 68512
www.iuniverse.com
1-800-Authors (1-800-288-4677)

Because of the dynamic nature of the Internet, any Web addresses or links contained in this book may have changed since publication and may no longer be valid.

The views expressed in this work are solely those of the author and do not necessarily reflect the views of the publisher, and the publisher hereby disclaims any responsibility for them.

ISBN: 978-0-595-45165-4 (pbk)
ISBN: 978-0-595-89475-8 (ebk)

Printed in the United States of America

For My Husband,
Dick
And My Sons,
Burke And Evan,
With Love

"… and still the Queen kept crying, "Faster! Faster."
—Lewis Carroll, Through The Looking Glass

Contents

ONE

BLOSSOMING IN WINTER

It is extraordinary,

my love, this second coming,
this sudden burgeoning into
a new season where once lay only
the dry promise of slowing senses
without energy to grow taut
against another possible dawn.

Let me remember spring

rather than face winter. Let me
recall my antic coming of age
in a flush of rebellion where I put
forth fierce blooms and stood high
and haughty over the placid daffodils.
I was young then. I could challenge
the sun and bask in my own reflection.

I thought my juices

could never be sapped nor
my roots loosen their grip on
the precarious earth I grew wild over.
I would ripen forever, the seasons
would stand still for me. I would
not, could not, be eclipsed.
When it was time, I would burn

Brightly forever on some solitary star.

But I tasted ashes, sweetheart,
and winter numbered my days.
You taught me to find comfort
in the root cellar and passion past
my prime. In your arms I savor
the slow shedding of petals
that blossom as they fall.

I celebrate our late becoming.

SLAUGHTER

I am grinding
the juniper berries,
bay leaf and pepper
in my mortar of milk glass
while you are
in the garage
with your kill.

A big buck this year,
brought down the first day
in light snow;
Now you must dress it
for the dinner table.
You don your surgeon's gloves
and pull down the door.
The carcass, already hung
yields to your fierce
assault on flesh and bone,
the hum of your fingers'
relentless precision.

That was hours ago.
Now it is dusk and your chores
of carnage are almost done.
I look out the kitchen window
past the rock garden.
I follow the trail of blood
past the weathered barn
where it stains the snow.
Next spring pinks and impatiens
will grow wild over the land
and erase the memory with
their own rush of crimson.

But now I grind
my juniper berries,
bay leaf and pepper
in my mortar of milk glass.
I will add a little red wine,
make a savory paste
for venison steaks.

Tonight we eat well.

DOLLARS AND CENTS

In our time

meaning is measured
by money. Legal tender
has replaced salvation
and love is weighed in karats.

That's the way it is.

We render our dreams
like chicken fat on stoves
bought with instant credit.
Lotto defines our souls.

So there it is, honey.

Don't blame me
if I've swallowed
the media message
to cash in, count up
and look out
for number one.

In our times
that's just the way it is.

CHERISH THE BONE

Like a felled oak
I have been stripped bare
and replanted into a dry bed,
my leg held high
and wrapped with wet
pandamus leaves
that smell of Phisohex.

The Druid medicos make their rounds
with probes and pronouncements
that would make their mothers proud
while tribe members wait
for their incantations,
their prophecy from trance.
Around me they do not dance
or perform miracles
but merely shake their heads
and move on to other beds
where they are held in greater awe.
Without a hele-stone
or bones of saints
what's left ...
shorthand on a chart;
a dash for cancer,
a dot for heart.

Tell me, my swollen limb,
my disordered extremity,
will I rise again or will they
call in the tree surgeon,
stack me for the fires?
Your rhythm, your blood surf
pound the answer home.

Get up and walk.
Cherish the bone.

AGING

Acts of God

leave no loopholes
for redemption.
Like a once proud city
leveled by a major quake
I have crumbled into
squalid disrepair.

Urban renewal

offers no quick fix
for shattered temples
scarred by fault lines.
My landscape defies
prodigious pruning
and suffers major blight.

Brittle bones
make shaky scaffolds
for ruins better left
to sink like Pompeii
into bedrock of better days
built long before the
hanging gardens fell.

and the worm turned.

9/11

"Mommy, the birds are on fire."

Self-propelled, they plummeted
From windows singly or in twos,
Unwilling comets trailing fire
That would take their breath
Away and change the world.

So said a little girl, high
On a Tribeca balcony
Watching the towers blaze
And tremble, splitting the sky
In their struggle to stand.

First casualties, these unsung
Heroes of dire circumstance
Would die in droves, anonymous
Innocents whose singular sin
Was chasing the American Dream.

That Tuesday morning disbelief
Turned to terror on the wings
Of a second plane zooming
In far too fast and too low to be
Another strike of pilot error.

It didn't waiver but seemed to focus,
Take careful aim before crashing
Into the face of the second Tower
Where fire from jet fuel
Would melt its very bones.

The City awoke to find downtown
A war zone without reason,
Fierce fact televised in living color
By anchormen too stunned to put
A spin on the unthinkable,

Or explain why so many workers,
Wall Street wizards to waiters
From Windows on the World
Would perish, detritus sacrificed
To the unholy hunger of a holy war.

A Jihad fermented in secret,
Distilled with messianic zeal,
Distorted by renegade Muslims,
Yet carefully calibrated, a hit
To surpass their wildest dreams.

And foil the City's finest,
A brotherhood of Firemen
And Police willing to risk all
To rescue those trapped within
And thwart the Tower's fall

Against all odds they climbed
Into the fiery eye of Tower Two
Trusting it would not blink or blow
Before they reached those caught
in the meltdown beyond the fire line.

But the Towers did not stand.
Built to endure hurricane force,
Their stiff outer skin kept them upright
Providing precious minutes for escape
But trapping the rescuers rushing in.

The soaring World Trade Center,
Icon of commerce in the only city
Big and brash enough to hold it,
Would implode with fury upon itself
And disappear in twenty seconds flat.

Leaving behind a killer cloud
Rushing from the epicenter headlong
Into spoked streets to fell vehicles
And pedestrians alike with breath
Foul enough to sicken the sun.

All New York wept as the world
Watched it momentarily stagger,
A mega-metropolis with attitude
Rising mightily to regain its swagger,
Trading its tears of raw rage for resolve.

A day that began like any other
With the great City sparkling in the sun
Would end as a metaphor for madness,
Solemnly observed and sanctified
By that little girl on a Tribeca balcony.

"Mommy, the birds are on fire."

PULLING BACK

I am pulling back, recoiling
to the safety of my ship.

Like a fisherman I reel
in my feelings and store
this most precious catch
in the snuggery of the hold.
Later I will clean them
like fluke or cod, chop
off their heads and gut
the silver flesh down to bone
exposing their fragility.

For like fish my
feelings took the bait,

ran with it, flashed through
the waves for the sheer joy of it
and relished every dangerous morsel.
They rose to the surface
with a hunger that risked the hook.
Deserting the deep they shot
to the surface with abandon, spurning
sanctuary and turning their backs
on the comfort of coral caves.

They paid dearly for
their run in the sun.

So now I must reclaim them,
gently tug them back from their dance
at the edge of the abyss.
I must recycle the debris
and free their mouths still
hooked on the kisses sirens sing of.
Trade-in time demands exchange
of wanton delicacies for the succor
and solace that cannot be found

in the white water
of my own designs

TRUMPET INTO POUNDING NAILS

Trumpet into pounding nails,
More bullets to blow Mr. Macy's holiday
To Kingdom come, shooting comets
And pinwheels blindly through
The suspended steel cables
Of the Brooklyn Bridge
Only to fizzle out and die over
The dark waters of the East River.

A night for stargazing reduced
to terror, transforming the sky-
Watchers into instant quarry
Caught between the cross-hairs
Of a madman's gun, once more
To be players in a holy war
Not of their making, a jihad
Playing out far from Mecca.

After 9/11 nothing
Will ever be the same.

I WANT TO LIVE WHERE LINDBERGH DIED

beyond the seventh pool
where the hairpin road
to Hana finally expires
having cut corners to cross
fifty-six coastal bridges
in dangerous disrepair.
Here, on this unrepentant
spit of land is where
I want to take final root.

Let this be my last outpost,
this tail-end of Maui where
the mongoose still hides
behind orchids to stalk
wild peacocks fanning
their tails at the sea.
Here, I can watch the sun
confront morning over Hana Bay
and melt the mists of Haleakala.

On the creamy sands of Hamoa
I can trade radio waves for surf,
focus instead on the sand crab
or shade my eyes to follow
the flight of iridescent birds
blinding to the city eye.
I will obey the sign tacked
onto the twisted Banyon tree
to brake for baby pigs.

Let me strike a bargain with Pele,
exchange worldly wisdom for
a final peace I can only forge
on this promontory of a planet
spinning out of control. Here
with you, the glow of dusk
heralds dawn and rhythms
of surf pound home daily
all the myriad reasons

of why I want to live
where Lindbergh died.

FOR TIM BELDIN

No monuments for men
who die in droves,
only piles of paper
stacked high with new
data on the dying
plus a possible square
on a quilt big enough
to cover an entire generation.

You did not go gentle into that
dark night rattling at your door.
No, you raged against the dawn
and cursed the sun for rising.
You shook your fist at God
and damned the doctors
who would not stop tracking
the end of a life not yet lived.

And there was always the Hell
you no longer believed in
waiting for you on the other side.
Wimpled, overwrought Sister Ignatius
had done her job well, etching in acid
through endless parochial school
afternoons the ultimate payback
for the likes of you and your ilk.

The last afternoon I saw you
I brought the four kingsize packs
of Camel Lights you asked for.
You were in the reserved hospice room
you had traded and paid for in blood,
foregoing the tulips in Amsterdam
one last time for a safe house instead
where you would finally die in a rented bed.

I shall miss you
In extremis.

WEDDING VOW

For you,

Evan and Paulette,
Today is a day to rejoice.
Seize it and celebrate.
Let your coming together
Be both shield and solace
Against uncertain seasons.

For mortality

Is sure as the tides
Ticking off the years
With seasonal persistence.
To share its passing
With one another is an act
Of love and great faith.

You met

In the first springtime
Of your lives. This afternoon
You join hands under
The high sun of summer
To proclaim the survival
And blossoming of that love.

Shout it out

To a world where isolation
Has become the norm.
Wear your vows as bold badges
Of your commitment. Display
Them proudly so all can
Delight in the love you share.

For together

You have reached this day
By holding on to the good dreams
In a world made uneasy by dreams.
You have created a climate
Where love can adjust to sudden
Squalls and rise to meet the sun.

No hothouse rose,

Your love, but rather a sturdy,
New blossom, a hybrid
Created to endure the orbiting
Of this uneasy planet.
May it put forth fierce blooms
Well into the autumn years.

For all

Of us who love you
And bask in your reflection
With such pride, today is a day
For renewal, for rekindling of dreams
We may once have held dear
And memories we thought lost.

We rejoice with you

And trace our reveries
On the map of your beginnings.
Together you have found
The question that answers
All the others. May your love
Carry you forth always

As it does today.

THEM

Why if
I have let go
Of the anger
At them,
The pure rage
At them,
The utter blame
Of them,
Why does the rage
Still reach meltdown
On those off days
When a flick
Of the wrist
Becomes a glove
Slapped against my soul,
A peremptory challenge
To do anything but
Turn the other cheek.

I will
Stand my ground
And fight to the death.
I will grind my teeth
Around the bone
That is them.
I will stoke my fury
In the furnace
That is them.
I will hone my hate
Against the grain
That is them.

I will not seek explanations
Or listen to definitions
That might soften
My stance or
Test my resolve
Against them

I will dig in my heels
And never let go.
I will never whine
Or whimper.
I will only rage
Against them.

Because it is
A question of survival,
You see. To win
Is to live and reign
Victorious over them.
Where I reside there
Is no middle ground,
No surface to steady
My feet or balm to salve
Old wounds inflicted
By them.

On those off days
When there is no
Sanity to regain,
No honorable retreat
And surrender
Is not possible,
It is then I must remember,
Must never forget
My malice knows no shame.

REVELATION

What a lie.

I have this fierce
new force in me—
young and firm of flesh
poised to break forth
onto new brinks
and grapple with dreams
left intact from before
the millennium.

Not likely at my age.

I feel superfluous like slang
that slipped out of usage
years ago. Only my heart
pumps on and on fueling
a body that long ago needed
to be hoisted onto the blocks
for a complete rehaul
and lube job special.

GRANDMOTHER

Gladys had a twinkle in her eye
as cold and distant as the north star.
To her husband who longed for
the warmth of the sun, she was
the far side of the winter moon, giving
herself to galaxies he could not dream of.

Her whale-bone collar stiffened
her suffragette spine as she marched
the streets in wrath disguised as dignity
carrying signs she penned in perfect Palmer
demanding the right to vote. Her descendents
were signed up for life-long temperance.

She kept a garden but her hands
were not gentle. The flowers grew
sickly and lived stunted; they knew
better than to die. She was a hoarder
hiding behind the collector's mask.
Her china all bore signs "Do Not Touch."

Dust dare not settle on one
of her eighty-four toothpick holders
or sixty salt cellars or the scrimshaw sent
by Uncle Judson who never did discover
gold in Alaska but found instead marriage
to Rose, the mother of Gypsy Rose Lee.

She threw nothing out. Not one issue
of the National Geographics piled
in the barn or the Civil War newspapers
moldering on the potting shed floor
next to the Special Editions of national
disasters like the Johnstown flood.

In the pantry could be found stacks
of neatly folded paper bags while
her parlor desk held a locked drawer
filled with faded newspaper clippings
and torn packets of rusty needles still
sharp as her tongue. She did not sew.

There were lanterns and sleigh bells,
brass, copper and china in triplicate,
chamber pots and a box full
of old pajama strings. She quit
the DAR for Marian Anderson
but never heard her sing.

She traced the family lineage on
a spidery tree whose roots reached
the Revolution. She was educated
when it was not fashionable and
worked when it was considered odd.
She did not put up peaches.

When her granddaughter came to visit,
she was taken on a tour of the town's
two competing funeral parlors where
Gladys examined slabs and caskets,
priced resting gowns and baskets
and learned the intricacies of embalming.

She was church-going Presbyterian
but preferred Spinoza, a Jew.
She wrote her own obituary knowing
it would appear on the front page
of the town's only newspaper.
They would name the Library after her.

When dead, she did not vacate
the premises easily. Her daughter
would open a drawer to face
a handwritten note, her mother's
voice still chiding ... "Helen,
please follow these instructions."

They were all signed simply, Mother.
Love would be superfluous, an indulgence
Gladys denied herself, although her daughter
remembered a time when as a child she had
posted letters to an unknown male cousin
on stationary that smelled of lavender.

No correspondence from him was ever
found in the voluminous boxes stored
in the attic that held every letter, postcard
and invitation she had ever received.
Finally, her letters were left ribbon-bound
but I know she does not rest in peace.

It would not suit her.

TRIPOD

Our daughter baptized you Tripod.
It fit; the perfect name for a big doe
with only three legs who could still leap
and bound up the hill to the old barn
with its peeling paint and falling-down
walls where we left out food each winter.

We first met you three years ago.
You lit up our landscape that winter
the snowfall broke all existing records.
You did not limp or hesitate but raced
with the others, the only sign, a shudder
of the shoulder that made us look twice.

It was the front, left leg, long lost
to a gunshot wound, we decided.
You had survived a careless hunter
and been able to discard the damaged limb,
possibly by chewing down to the bone
to emerge with your grace in tact.

The next winter you returned to us,
followed closely by a fawn, its legs
still unsure and wobbly in the snow.
You led them all, Tripod, nudging
out the competition, young bucks
who could learn by your lead.

It is again winter and the first snow
has fallen. As always, food is left up
at the decrepit barn so in need of repair.
We expect to see you soon, Tripod,
secure in the knowledge that no hunter
would dare bring home a three-legged deer.

TO EVAN, THIS IS NOT AN APOLOGY

To Evan, this is not an apology
or an explanation, but ...

So you got caught in the crossfire
of words we hurled like stones
at each other, your father and I.
I wish I could say, thank you
for telling me—I needed to know
but I don't feel that way at all
when I am forced to open the door
just a crack on my cellar days.

Listen to me carefully.

I did not tie them up with ribbons,
those days, or pack them away
in some bottom drawer of my soul
next to the fading stack
of all my hell-bent ways
just so I could tally up
and check their toll on all
of us at some later date.

Believe me, there was no intent.

My sins were unplanned—
sowed in innocence with no
regard for DNA—blind seeds
hungry to blossom, eager
to grow straight into the eye
of the sun. I did not fear
overexposure then or listen
to any heartbeat but my own.

Not even yours.

Certainly not your father's,
a man I married because it
was time; it was the thing to do
and I, crowd-pleaser that I am
chose the aisle rather than
acknowledge a heart that didn't
skip a beat on the way
to the altar. Not a beat.

Did I know, you ask.

I was not stupid but tunnel vision
and fractured focus bent the days
to fit my dreams of the moment.
And I had many; I wore them
like out-of-date hats, odd angled
badges to live or die by.
Lip service was not my style.
I craved commitment like candy.

And yes, I drank.

Like my father before me
and yours before you;
because it hid me from hard eyes
and softened the sharp tongues.
With waters bottled by Lethe& Co.
I could toast a life marginally lived
and be the star of home movies
I watched alone in an empty house.

But I knew the little lies.

The thorny ones that daily rushed
into the lush landscape that hid
the house you grew up in,
that still sting my eyes when I turn
around to view those brambled years
that almost did me in, along with
the two sheep in your father's
swimming pool—the pool he dug daily.

I'm sure you remember

that angry wall, reinforced by his case
of Budweiser, digging, digging—
daring us to tell him it wouldn't work.
After claiming the sheep and chicken coop
his pool became the grave we never
mentioned. Finally, it was the lawn
you and your brother wouldn't mow.
We swam at Tohickan Creek

And yes, we fought

Through those forever years in voices
heard above the breaking glass.
The little lies blossomed—deadly
and enormous—taking all of our time,
straining our nerves, draining our days.
I thought the neighbors didn't know
and alone, I told myself that you
and your brother didn't notice.

I know now that you did.

BECAUSE

Because I loved you

I have tried to accept
the unacceptable even
though it diminished me
to the vanishing point.

Because I loved you

I have tried to fathom
the unfathomable even
as it pushed me past
the last limits of reason.

Because I loved you

I have tried to fit myself
into your puzzle of despair
only to be jig-sawed into a
landscape not of my making.

Because I loved you

I have tried to upturn
the world and defy gravity
only to lose my balance
and fall off the edge.

Because I loved you

I have spoken the unspeakable,
to one unable to hear
that where I craved commitment,
all I spelled was diversion.

THE BONE CHAPEL

In this walled Portuguese town,
Apollo's temple to the sun shares
space with an overwrought cathedral,
piled stone upon laborious stone,
a monument to Caesar's final fall.

Our earnest young guide explains,
this chapel where we stand cloistered
was painstakingly constructed
from sacred relics, the boncs
of former priests and friars.

My husband, ever the surgeon,
always the prickly anatomist,
identifies a bent and scarred femur
tightly packed against the curved
edge of a small, chipped radius.

An overweight wimpled nun
kneels painfully and genuflects
while fourth graders in her charge,
uniformed and neat in navy blue,
nudge each other giggling.

Caveat Emptor, I buy a candle
for my father who left the Church
but still crossed himself in dreams.
A camera flash exposes sudden
graffiti on an almost toothless skull.

Maria a Manuel "93."

THE DAY YOU WERE BORN

For Olivia

The day you were born
was the third time, Olivia,
I have been granted a day
to hold dear and glorify.
The first was a cold, wet Friday
in November when your Daddy
was born after many, many hours.
He came forth and my heart sang.
I kniew somewhere the Magi gave
thanks and a singular star blazed.

Your Uncle Evan woke me
with a kick at two in the morning
on a starless October eve. Still
nudging against me, so eager
to be born, unwilling to wait,
we rushed into the streets to find
a cabdriver who heeded our warning.
He ran red lights and disregarded
traffic to reach Lenox Hill. Hospital
in time for my second epiphany.

The day you arrived, sweet Olivia,
your daddy called late at night.
Your birth was imminent, he said.
We drove too fast through rain
threatening to become ice,
arriving in time to hold you
and celebrate your beginnings.
The labor or your coming had left your
parents' limp but their love shone bright
to see your radiance challenge the night.

A granddaughter to love and cherish,
my third epiphany and greatest gift.

PARK ROW

He sits on the sidewalk
cross-legged near my office,
a cardboard sign balanced
precariously on his lap.
Green felt-tip letters
shakily spell out ...
VETERAN ... AIDS ... HUNGRY
... GOD BLESS YOU ...

With many others
I pass him daily.
Gaunt, but clean shaven
with matched socks,
he has on occasion
brought a small dog
he cradles in his arms.
For three years now
I have watched him
haunt the seasons
on downtown streets.
For some weeks he had TB
but that passed. Still,
his bones rattle in winter.
He has a room somewhere,
an SRO perhaps to keep out
the demons when night
sweeps his sidewalk bare.
He is not offensive.
He does not stop me
in my tracks like the
teenage girl with open sores

on her legs who sits
with her little girl
against the wall of the diner
where I sometimes lunch.
To her, I have given ...
because she is a child
who has a child of her own,
because it hurts too much
to pass her by and be left
to examine my own heart.
The veteran does not rate
my money. When it is late
or raining and I'm dead tired,
I hear myself mouth words
I don't dare articulate ...
get a job, I whisper only
to myself and invariably
taste the bile of shame.

This city where I grew up,
a city I love, has changed
with the times. It wears
a harsh new face.
The secret places to hide
are gone as is the solace
the city was known for.

Since 9/11 we hurry on our way.
We no longer make eye-contact.

UP AND DOWN

Up is as high
as the stars
over Hana Bay.
Down is as low
as Daddy dying.
Up is the birth
of my babies,
who promise salvation.
Down is dread
of an empty house
and a cold dry bed.

Up or Down,
In or Out,
my life hangs
by a thread,
its sharp edges
exposed and open.
There are no panaceas
to ease the way
or soften the blows
that drive me
on any given day.

LAST WORD

Words excite
from first babble
to last rhetoric
and all discourse
in-between where
I spent years
in empty translation.

Married on a whim
while riding the waves
of style I lost
my best years
to a high-fat diet
of poetry without
rhyme or reason.

Now in my dotage
I spend time with
my thesaurus matching
out-of-date usage
with out-of-mind
definitions I lost
years ago when

words were the keys
that primed my passion.

HEART FAILURE

It was same day surgery.

A minor procedure
still fraught, however,
with implications
of the knife.

They had taken my teeth

along with my dignity.
I was left surgically swaddled
and guerneyed in a gown
too small with no snaps.

The clues to my identity

had been seized—my Timex watch
and garnet ring relinquished.
Anonymous and expendable
I was now a cipher in a system

that suddenly discovered

the EKG done the day before
with such brisk efficiency
in concert with other pre-op tests
had registered a blip, an infarct

on the computer readout

of my life that signaled
a past heart attack,
a jot on the zigzag map
of life's contingencies.

Just over-read I was told,

by an overzealous machine
that is never careless ...
it means nothing, they repeat
as they wheel me in.

With luck, tomorrow is another day.

ANNIVERSARY

A day like any other

except I remember the color
of July, the dance of rain
on your broken umbrella ...
held high, elbow-spoked over
our heads where we listened
to it tap its heels for us alone.

A day like any other

except it was the first of many
to follow the pattern of perennials
we set for ourselves, to root
and throw off seasonal blooms
to match the progress of our days,
the changing climate of our love.

A day like any other

except it was our buoy of hours,
our divining rod of sudden storms.
Who could have guessed, my love,
that the hours and days would become
rungs of a ladder reaching for stars
put out just for us to hang our love on.

WHO WOULD HAVE GUESSED, SWEETHEART

Who would have guessed, sweetheart

that at our age we could
couple with such grace
or find more than solace
in each other's arms?

You have stirred up dreams

that lost their sting years ago,
made them star-driven again,
prying them like mollusks
from the bottom of my pool
to sail like petals on the surface
of a consciousness I thought I'd lost.

Oh yes, my love …

you've done more than just
fill space and juggle time.
You've made my spirit soar
and my tired old body sing.

When the sun is high

above your beloved garden,
over land you love and work
so hard, I wait in the kitchen,
listening for your footsteps,
ready to reap what you sow
and silently reflect on how

very much I love you.

FINALLY, LOVE

For too many years
I loved only those
unable to return it.

My mother

enamored by corporate ladders
briefly embraced the suburbs
and motherhood to assure
herself she was one of the girls.
She quickly returned to work.
Nurturing was not in her portfolio.

My father

drank, then too soon died.
But in between curled up
in his lap while he read to me
from Homer and Kipling,
I breathed love's possibility
and became an addict.

My husband

of twenty years substituted charm.
for love. I rose to the bait,
swallowing whole the words we
flung at each other for decades.
Rage and spite measured
the distance of our days.

But you

my love, have come to me
at our calendar's end
when days are precious.
You have leapt walls
to take my breath away
and revive my tired old heart.

You have made me a true believer.

PRISONER OF WORDS

Let me out of this rattling matrix
where words war with one another
and collide between falling stars
to battle the cosmos and rock
my boat of store-bought sleep.

Let me join you in your garden
my love, where you coerce the soil
to sow your seeds throughout a realm
where language has no dominion,
and the rose and rutabaga rule.

Let me scatter my sins and relieve
my angst against the even rows
of summer corn deaf to syntax.
Grant me the peace of hard, daily
toil that breaks the fever of dreams.

WINNING

In this tug of war
There are no winners.

We are in over our heads.
Mired in certainty,
Our heels dug in
On opposite sides
Of the bottom line,
We battle on and on.

We summon every ounce
Of dark energy from a lifetime
Reservoir of slights,
Real or imagined,
Driven by the knowledge
That losing is a little like death.

II this tug of war
There are no winners.

A LETTER YOU NEVER READ, MOTHER

But should have.

It was not written until your death
bestowed the necessary grace,
a benediction that limited your power
and monitored the reach of your arm
from the grave where it could
so easily grab my ankle,

And did daily,

even after my then husband sprinkled your ashes—
conveniently shipped in a cardboard container
shaped rather like an oatmeal box—onto our neighbor's
sheep meadow. I did not tread any light fantastic
of the soul or find peace without your daily calls.
Your grip did not slacken or give an inch.

It died no easier than you had.

I wish I could say I now forgive you,
that time has healed the running wound
to finally bridge the gap that during our
lifetime was an impassible span—a chasm
to catch our words and reverberate
their intent against us without respite.

But I cannot.

I can only say that time does not soothe
the primal years when I cut my milk teeth
on your hard edges. I cannot forgive what
was never there or forget what was never given.
My hindsight does not expiate old sins—it offers
only justice that is final and fiercely forged.

Apocalypse was never easy, Mother.

SIT-IN: 1968

There were thirteen of us,
concerned parents all,
who answered the call
to occupy P.S. 41
an elementary school
in Greenwich Village.
We were there to make a stand,
to support community control
of city schools, a grand design
but a Civil Rights issue still,
short on civility but not overkill.
We were there to demand
that all the schools shut down
by Union lock-out open up
and teach our children again—
both the black and the white.

We would sit tight
with Ocean Hill-Brownsville,
a black poverty pocket
in the far reaches of Brooklyn
which few of us had heard of,
much less visited. Oh, yes,
but we had answered the call,
would add our voices to support
a community looming large
in the public eye, where every day
Media head-lined another lie.
We would fight the good fight
with our brothers and sisters,
join hands, and share their plight.
We were now inside our school
and committed to staying the night.

We were a diverse group,
our offspring the common ground
we would fight for to the death
now that we were honor bound.
We boasted a Methodist minister
and two doctors, one a medico,
the other, an erudite PH.D.
Five women and eight men committed
to opening the school by whatever means.
We did not know each other well.
Our group, the Concerned Parents
was born of the crisis, split from the PTA,
promised to gain the moral high ground
and hold it. We were all over thirty,
energized and angry, happy to have a cause
in that decade where causes were held holy.

I was not part of the midnight takeover
but the next morning calls went out to
Concerned Parents throughout the village …
"Get to the school, they're being busted."
I ran with my oldest son to stand firm.
A corner school door opened. A loud whisper
called me in. They needed a child, a symbol
to meet the press who were already
beginning to gather. My son wanted
to go home The flashbulbs hurt his eyes
and he had to pee. But he didn't cry.
With the arrival of my husband
the Photo-op was over but the damage
was done. My son's gaze followed us
from TV or stared at us through handcuffs
from the front page of the Village Voice.

The Sit-in lasted six days and we had won.
The school would open. The deed was done.
Victory might jump-start community control.
Our sit-in displayed the sudden idealism
of Village parents yet was middle-class
in its marrow. Several people got drunk,
Dinners were delivered from Peter's Backyard.
My son did not have his annual birthday party
and later transferred to another first grade.
He was known. His picture attained icon status,
For me, the sit-in will always be caught
in the angry words of a well-dressed women
who yelled up to me as I sat in the window.
She raised her fist, rage contorting her face,
"You scab; I hope you die of cancer."

It was our last day and the time
had come to finally go home.

WORDS WITHOUT END

Your words last night
Were knives digging deep
Into flesh already scarred
and intent only on healing.

They flew at me without end,
Staccato thrusts, parried
by a zealous D'Artignian
determined to win at any cost.

Yes, your words
left me licking old wounds
already bled and tasting of salt
from tears too often shed.

Your words were not ones
I could turn off with a switch.
No, they beat down upon my ears
like rain that wouldn't stop.

I cannot forget last night's
words today. They hang
between us now, another barrier
keeping us each from the other.

Your words last night
cut me to the quick. I wish
you had weighed them before
you let them fall like stones

into a deepening pool
to form concentric circles,
prisoners of a ripple effect
seeking but never reaching shore.

Your words last night
were better left unsaid.

I LOST MYSELF ALONG THE WAY

When you have married
more than once,
you wear new names
until they fail and fray,
losing their letters like buttons
on last season's new shirt
waiting to be thrown away.

The name you carried with you,
learned to write in script
and used to translate dreams,
the one you whispered,
held dear as yours alone,
the only one you fully own
has been lost along the way.

Now your name has gone missing.
It is locked tight in memory boxes
that no longer open or resurface,
that have forgotten how to spell.
Men retain the privilege of their name;
it is theirs to perpetrate but two-time
losers can forgo their name forever.

THE MAGDALENA LAUNDRIES

For All Who Toiled There

Mortal sin was the get-in-free card
for all who became wards of the State,
consigned without trial to toil endless hours
in a labyrinth of laundries built set up by fate
under Mary Magdalene's convent gate.

Sins, mortal or venial, were the keys
to unlock the rooms of sulfurous fumes
where hard labor taught modesty and grace.
There, the great vats were primed daily
to be never empty or slow their relentless pace.

The good sisters knew all sins were equal,
whether for the victim who spread her legs
at the first blow or the shy youngster
with sashay hips. and a come-on smile.
It mattered not a bit, for all sins were vile.

Made legal by contract with the Archdiocese,
the convent was a dread depository for girls
who told lies, wore lip-gloss or asked why.
All daughters were welcome to boil the sheets,
to contemplate their sins while still on their feet.

Wimpled witches they were, these holy nuns
of the Magdalena Order, pinching breasts
and exploring the privates of supplicants
who had lost the battle in their home parish
and been sentenced to scrub their lives away.

Many would live out their years in service
to the sisters, their days ever devoted
to the dirty work of others, their night lost
in feverish lip-service to God, while sweet sleep
came only after hours of compulsory prayer.

Their hair fell out or turned white praying
to the Holy Mother on swollen knees.
They sought intervention. Or a Miracle.
A sizable donation to the order might buy
Absolution or a Dispensation to set them free.

But leaving the convent was not encouraged.
by nuns who saw justice in supervised baths.
The wicked must accept their evil ways
and show gratitude to the habited gargoyles
who monitored them through endless days.

They would confess, these young women
without method or means to deny sins
sown in innocence, free and pure as air.
They would weep into the vats, their tears
daily penance for the lives spent there.

Can it be a crime when Church and State
conspire in the name of righteousness
to strip young maids of their maidenhood?
The answer, lost to parish records lies buried in,
archived deletions made for the common good.

Without rhyme or reason to justify the deed,
the nuns found solace in the ancient holy screed
and the words of sundry priests who came
to praise their unfailing charity, their holy duty
to those consigned to wash away their shame.

THE DAY YOU DIED

For Ryan Halligan

The day you died

The sun had trouble rising
And will never again
Seem to shine so bright.
It was a day of desolation
For the many who loved you,
Who broke under the pain
Of your long goodnight.

The day you died

Time stopped, a dire plight
Signaling forever a change
In the singular ways we live
Out our days. We must learn
To monitor our memories,
Stop ourselves from asking why
You who gave so much did die..

The day you died

I recalled your myriad gifts,
Some by nature double-edged.
Your very sweetness promised
A vulnerability and trust that
Challenged the bully, the outcast
To go after you, you who would
Rather make friends than fight.

The day you died

Was one of monumental grief,
Of loss beyond any promise of relief.
Words could not measure the light
In your eyes or the distance
Of your smile and the spell it cast.
We must remember when the heart
Breaks, the joy you spread, Ryan

Will last and last and last.

IT BROKE MY HEART

It broke my heart

to discover Freud snorted coke
and hid bottles beneath his bed.
For this, my father left the Church
to worship at the post-modern altar
of secular saints while I was led
down the twisty, primrose path
to seek the bitter truth of secrets
better left in silence or unsaid.

It broke my heart

to read the letters Freud wrote
to his friend and colleague, Fliess,
whose very special expertise bespoke
of the unknown powers of the nose.
It was there the psyche happily resided,
not the mind so full of blind spots
and recesses where magic arose.
Didn't Dr. Freud agree?

It broke my heart

when the good doctor relaxing
after a taxing day at the couch,
agreed with vigor. He declined,
however, to publish. The sharp
Vienna air cleared his sinuses
so he could heed the good advice
of those who, thank God, knew better,
who now viewed him with dismay.

It broke my heart

to realize I had too quickly jumped
into the quirky quagmire of analysis,
bared my soul and sought absolution
at the feet of a true Freudian believer.
We would parse, cut and dice my life
for my allotted hour with little progress.
Now I wish I'd opted for a splashy First
Communion with Confession on the side.

BELLEVUE

1. WRISTS

How placid they are
In their nudity
Without bracelets or even Timex
To stem their fragile tides.
So harmless.
Two crossed Modigliani necks
Regarding each other … waiting.

2. SEVENTH FLOOR

Because it is Sunday,
A Sabbath for judges and the lord,
I am penned on the Seventh Floor
Where they keep the wild
And uncannily mild.
I am left in a crowd of empty ones
Strait-jacketed to beds
With wired heads or pacing the halls.
The Seventh Floor is the doomsday ward,
A canyon of judgment and apocalypse
With steep walls and no way out
But through a door marked No Exit.

Nurses like big-breasted turkeys
Fan their feathers in a glass cage
And pretend not to hear the knocks
Of the mad who bleed their knuckles
For kicks and attention.
Big, deaf Butterballs,
A butcher's delight,
The nurses shift at night
Pecking the bodies that feign sleep
In the bed lined corridors.

The hall is Avenue A,
A common ground for rest and rendezvous
Where cells like Sunday shops
Are shuttered and locked.
Among these crazed shells
From which the snails
Fled long ago I am left.

At the corridors dead-end a teenage girl
Tattoos herself with a hidden pin
While conversing with a secret lover.
Another chews her skin
While still another
Performs a stately solitary dance
Like an aging debutante.

I have been set down here,
Checked and mated.
My demands are met
For solace and self-protection.
No one has anything to fear
For my anger has been scattered
And meticulously pecked away.

They will let me
Stew in the others' juice
Until I'm done.
They've won.

3. NUN'S LAMENT

It was her secret;
Whether she had left the convent
By an act of will or been expelled
For bodily sins of attrition
Was an unanswered question
She locked behind eyes shuttered
Like the confessional, blind impassioned
Eyes set in a bisque china-doll face.
By the heavily screened ward windows
She rubbed her wedding finger raw
With loss, for she had been a Bride
Of Christ and the Divorce had left
Her spirit split, forced her to become
A double-edged Magdalene
Fingering sacred relics made
From scraps found on the floor.
She thought every meal a communion
And reunion where warehouse bread
Hid sacrificial wafers and Dixie cups
Held only twice blessed wine.
So she wasted self in prayer
Walking the Stations of the Cross
With beads of knotted string
Awkward without their familiar ring.
Her Aztec Christ demanded apostate blood ...
He was remote and fierce with no pax
Vobiscums offered for her incantations.

She was found Sunday morning
Under the bathroom sinks
With a hand-honed mirror blade
She had held close and hidden
For the final act of cleansing.
Blood finally attested to her purity
For the final vows.

4. E.C.T

They would shock her into sanity.
In November they had her wired,
The words died in the cathedral
Of her mouth. Her hair reversed
The spin from gold to straw
And mixed with the dry leaves
Dying beyond the meshed windows.

In April they had finished.
She was left short-circuited
With empty sockets once filled
With diamonds now reduced to coal.
Her voice which once held wonder
No longer reached for high notes
Or raced to outwit the hare.
It trembled, a mutant nightingale
Unable to sing or even shrill a scream.

Cauterized brain cells
Led her through peeling halls
With measured shuffles in shoes
Twice-borrowed and too big.
Her glass slippers had been tagged
And locked in cold storage.
Her body grew in inverse ratio
To a mind lost and dieted to death.

She ate quantities of bread
And pounced on potatoes she hid
Like jewels in her pockets.
She had a husband but the money
Ran out with his patience

Although he sent occasional fruit.
She attacked the oranges like wounds
And saved their skins like so many scabs
Of broken blood in her pillowcase.

They never did turn to gold.

5. SOLITARY

There were three of us in the sealed room
Reserved for the uncooperative mad.
Punished for my get-me-out-of-here phone call
I shared my insulated tomb with two others.
One was a woman, bandaged and immense
Strapped to a wheeled gurney she breathed
Into constant motion with her fractured moans
And heaving bones. Two was a Bowery whore
Still caressing a past of red velvet
And private parties. The one hamstrung
And bound, when she spoke at all, shrilled
Octaves of pain that strained her bonds
And shattered our ears like fine crystal.
The bewildered prostitute bounced
Off the walls like a red-light balloon
Pausing only to drawl disjointed threats
She dropped like pig Latin pearls
For us to string together and decipher.
My fears flew, a swarm of bees circling,
Each with a separate sting to remind me
Of all the things I'd done to wind up here.
One paced and bounced while the other
Smashed her gurney against the leather door
Testing its limits by sheer will of raging voice.

Screams and knocks
Brought no response
But it did make the rats
Jump in their corners.

6. THERE ARE NEEDLES IN MY EYELIDS

She lay in the next bed
For we slept barracks style.
She was a spirit of mixed origins
Speaking in tongues, her words a salad
Of Spanish, English and Indian.
She had no rest at night, a private
Drafted into this mad army,
Who endured needles in her eyelids
That would not let her retinas rest.
Before these eyes the enemy
Continually battled and tormented her
With threats of death and damnation.
At times she was in their camp,
A prisoner under house arrest
While we gained uneasy status
And became her interrogators.
She could not blink or wink us away.
She kept us awake with confession
While shouting our secrets
To the commanders of the ward.

She talked to the walls
And marched the halls
With pinned open eyes
That could not turn off
The endless war she had to fight.
She was the mascot
And bugler of our plight
And she had opted for eternal sight.

7. DANCE

I was not the guest of honor
At this ball of masked minds
Where drugged patients came
One night a week to meet and retreat
In a parody of dance. Left here by
Dire accident. I was a flower pinned,
Against the wall behind a wheelchair
While slippered feet tapped out
Long forgotten steps in time
To Guy Lombardo oldies.

Men lined one side
Of the gymnasium.
Women the other.
They eyed each other
Through secondhand balloons
And used crepe streamers
That jump-started their
Shell-shocked visions
Into a frenzy of Twist
And distorted Hustle.

Women danced with women;
They danced alone.
They performed solos
With their rough robes
Flowing like Isadora's.
The men circled,
Clutching the tops
Of their pajama bottoms
Only to let them drop ...
And be escorted to the 7th Floor.

Promises were exchanged for cigarettes
And tentative touches for cups
Of Hawaiin punch laced with tears.
I watched, swallowing my own gall,
A dancer at this mad Mardi Gras.
When it was over we were marched
Back to the wards, then to bed,
Medicated and left for dead
Until next week when we would again
Dance to the tunes in our own heads.

8. MOVIE

They have a theater here.
During the week doctors interview
Patients and present case histories
To medical students. They expose
Bone and vein, probe points of pain
And prod the asylum residents
Who wince obligingly. On cue.
The doctors are educators
Who don't learn from eye contact.
They are not devotees of cinema.

Wednesday nights are different,
A study in contrasts, a counterpoint
Where patients march right in
Holding out their symptoms
To be stamped like tickets.
Their complaints cover them
Like costly furs as they wave
And wait for the film to begin.
Giggling, they trade autographed
Notes they penned themselves.

The patients understand
The cutout world of celluloid
Better than the medicos.
So much larger than life
With grand scale conflicts
And heart-stopping pratfalls,
They share the hero's secrets, lament
With the betrayed wives and shake
Their fists at the villain. They see
Eyeball to eyeball with Bette Davis.

The inmates already know
What the doctors never will.
Flesh and blood may fail
But they can still dance
With Charlie's little tramp.

9. INTERVIEW

He was there to
Examine my stigmata
And probe my frontal lobes.
He held me in his hand the way
My son holds a caterpillar.

He was my judge
This fat psychiatrist
Spreading over his desk
Like rising dough oozing
Between stacks of manila folders.

He fingered my file
Whittling my life down
Into neat little piles
To mix with the ashes
Of his exploding cigar.

He could put me back
Into that folder,
Pin me forever,
A Monarch among moths
Unable to beat my wings.

Finally he snapped shut
The file and told me
I could go home.
I left reluctantly,
Sane and alone.

TWO

SUPERMAN

Look
Up in the sky
It's a bird
It's a plane
It's Superman
alias
Daddy.

You never knew.
It was classified.
Hoover himself sent
her to the altar
in a coded veil
with a vial hidden
in her bridal bouquet
of babies' breath
and portent camellias ...
a pretty ploy to outwit
my poor Clark Ken t
whose business suits
were tailored to hide
muscle and break bone.
I knew you could leap
tall buildings with
a single bound if she'd
stop lacing your scotch
with kryptonite so you
tripped on every step
instead of soaring through
the sky tagging jets
as you were destined.

She knew it all, Daddy …
the rocket that brought you
and the swaddling cloth
that was made to fit
you like a wet suit.
She kept it in a box
marked Bloomingdale's
on the top shelf of her closet
with old hats and empty
trees without shoes.
I wanted to tell you …
when you tossed me in the air
like a basketball and caught
me like a helium balloon
in your steel arms.

I knew you had X-ray vision
that summer Sunday in Amagansett
when you ordered the three-inch
splinter stabbing my heel
from my foot leaving
it free to fit any shoe.
I knew when she par-boiled
your tropical fish in the tank
built over the radiator …
you came home to find
their see-through bodies
and fishnet fins floating
on top of the water,
bald-eyed with mouths
open for the hook.
The guppies, the zebras,
the plaidies were all quite dead …
so much antipasto for the cat.

Her apology was ash
In her mouth and she hooded
her eyes against your gaze.
She knew I knew
but if I told she would
have cut out my tongue
and kept it in the jar
of kosher pickles
you were so fond of.
She kept the kryptonite
in the canister marked salt
and nightly dealt near lethal doses.
She ordered twin beds
from Sloans; she feared
the strength she drained daily.
But I did play tricks …
leading you to phone booths
and amusement parks
where you were faster
than any bullet.

You just never knew, Daddy,
what a real bitch Lois Lane was.

WHEN I WAS TWENTY

When I was twenty
I was still a virgin ...
an overripe apple
waiting to be picked.
M. not only picked me;
he ate me core and all
for I was dying to be tasted.
I knew he had a portrait
somewhere like Dorian Gray
with wrinkles and warts
and evil tattoos
on a lascivious frame.
But I was twenty
and love was carnal
and his body a
wonder to behold.

We made love on my studio couch
tasting each others' tongues
and our body's salt
before there were wounds.
We made love in the shower
under the stinging water
that helped our hands
find the way.
We made love in
the old fashioned tub
with clawed feet
that could barely
accommodate one.
We made love on the fire escape

only to come in branded
with stripes of rusty iron.
We made love on the rooftop
under the Manhattan sky
that never turns to pitch.
We made love in front
of the fire, turning ourselves
on a spit that glowed
with our embers.

We made love in front
of the full length mirror
and watched our faces
fulfill the fantasy.
We made love
in Washington Square,
Central Park and the old
Loews's Palace Theater
across the street from
St. Vincent's Hospital.

We made love continually …
Sometimes frantic … fast like
the shooting star I imagined
he fell from, other times slowly
with care learning each others' bodies …
his hard inner thigh, the flat belly.
My breasts would peak
and he would roar into me
more powerful than any locomotive,
murmuring in French …
I was his petit choux,
his caviar, his icing on the cake.

I was very edible and he
had beautiful teeth
and a tongue that fit
my mouth like a lollipop.

But sweets get eaten
or thrown away,
melting into memories
to be measured
against the present day
when my best offer
will be to remember
when I was twenty
and love was carnal
and I was still a virgin ...
an overripe apple
waiting to be picked.

REBUTTAL

I can turn you off
Like a radio
With a flash of my eyelid.
Wireless,
I direct like radar.
I aim my lens,
Old lightening pole
To render ash, ash
And a bone or two
Splintered against eye-slits
That no longer elect
To be threaded or needled
By your glance,
Your bloody eyes.

You had your chance
That unraveled day in May
To eat me like a sugar baby.
I was spun sugar,
I was cotton candy
Willing to melt between
Your lips and sweeten
The blows of ax
And jackhammer alike.
You had your chance
To lick your lips
And let me go
But chose to maintain
The status quo.

So now I turn you off
Sweet soul assassin.

I am no longer edible.

LADY OF THE FLOWERS

I am the lady of the flowers,
of ranting marigolds
and too lush peonies.
I neglect my duties to reflect
on my own blossoming
and designate floral designs
for devotees of clinging vines.
Babies are mere clover
to be chewed upon
by complacent cows rattling
on in communal pastures.

As for me, I demand
perfect pots and nourishment
too heady for the common plot.
Rich soil is needed and daily care,
the company of maidenhair
and prodigious pruning
if I am to flourish.

I make a rare hot-house bloom,
stunning to look at for my own sake.
What does it matter if I
cannot reproduce my own?

WHAT SHALL I WEAR TODAY, ODYSSEUS?

Every morning before
the rest have risen,
before the sun unlocks
another empty day,
I sit at my loom
to pluck my nerves bare,
dear Odysseus.
The root question
never varies but is always
the same ... what shall
I wear today, my love?
The loom is badly in need
of repair and my broad bones
are broken and barren
having been worked over
by the hooves that
paw me nightly.
Worthy stallions,
hoof-handed and heavy
they trample my flesh while
you cavort with the whore of Troy.
I won't be a nagging wife
but what shall I wear?
what fabric shall I turn out?
for all and sundry
to hail or hoot at ...
something captivating,
a chemise to challenge
the slanting eyes of youth
or a kimono complete with fan

to hide my faltering age.
Perhaps a gown of golden mesh
to ensnare the keepers of my
empty womb while you
cavort with the whore of Troy.

What shall I wear today, Odysseus?

MY MAFIA LOVER

I must annihilate you

Towering Mafia man.
You gunned me down and bedded
Me with bullets that summer
When I was numberless as yet,
An intact zero with virgin eyes
That sought your thighs
To flood the empty tide.

Oh, how you accommodate.

Boss Man, you were too generous.
You mapped my future on flesh just
Breaking from its granite cowl.
You with your calloused mechanic's
Hands so apt at alchemy
Melted my stone to blood
That crested on command.

You manipulate too well

My consigliore. Your trigger
Fingers played me like a precision
Instrument, a deadly Lugar perhaps
That could explode and dash my eyes ...
Snap the ties that leashed me to your bed.
I may well have died that summer
You fused the wires in my head.

You anticipate too much

Sleek capo of my mad, sad days.
I was your table, your cushioned chair,
Beat up and roughened with wear.
No more will I be the furniture
Of your life, sadly in need of paint.
Underneath, I'm Chippendale
And will marry a saint

Do not implicate me

In your schemes dear hit man.
I am not a fig to be sucked dry.
You have already torn my flesh
And thrown away the fruit.
Now, get out. Let me do penance,
Become a nun; my hair will be shorn,
I'll make friends with the sun.

FOR BURKE AT 15

When I was fifteen
my Mother wore too much
makeup and bore down
on my friends with
non-stop anecdotes
and cookies she didn't bake.
She didn't know her place
like our maid who stayed
out of sight in the kitchen
baking cookies to establish
my mother's generosity.

Why didn't she play bridge?
afternoons with other mothers
who kept out of sight?
holing up at the PTA
or Women's Club,
only coming home
to fix dinner and offer
a perfunctory kiss good night?

But no ...
she wore dirndls
and peasant blouses.
She pierced her ears
and laughed too loud
at fifteen-year-old wit
she didn't understand.

My friends and I talked
in a code she'd never crack.

I could have died.

NEVER FIRST

Villanelle for Evan at 13

How can you ever forgive your brother?
His birth left you second-hand, always last,
Yet can there ever be another?

Who knows you so well behind the eyes?
Or charts your days to share your past.
How can you ever forgive your brother?

He had the first job, was the first to find
Girls, taste their lips, hold them fast,
Yet can there ever be another

Who will be of your blood and bone?
Who'll read your thoughts when you're alone
How can you ever forgive your brother?

You are still shorter than your Mother
While he has grown tall, a tree of a man.
How can you ever forgive your brother
Yet can there ever be another?

DON'T BUY ME A FEATHER DOWN BED

Don't buy me a feather down bed
high on a circular rotunda;
seventeen jewels to murder
my minutes, chopping off
their heads to be caught
in the baskets that hold
all of time's leftovers.

Let me defy Einstein and Newton.
Let me keep my hours with you
fresh as newly cut flowers.
I will display our love
in clay flower pots
and cut-glass urns ...
I will never let it die.

See those roses there
with their petals peeling,
left from the beginning before
their thorns made me bleed.
I prefer peonies, lush with
secrets, whose deep roots
cling to earth and stone.

Big and moonfaced, petaled
to grasp how soft a touch
must be, your fingers held
just a trace of flowers
to be memory-pressed
in root and bone.
Forget all the rest.

Just save one lily for me.

IN MEMORIAM: HART CRANE

You saw the daughter of Powhatan beat
footprints on her father's drum,
a dance for braves to catch a white man's head.
You met Van Winkle halfway cross the Bridge
which double-crossed its shadow
onto Panama and bled.

Threadbare, suspended by the welder's thumb

you swept dumb docks to share a seaman's bed;
rocked and rolled with a sailor boy
who belched apocalypse is dead.
Stiff-necked saint, squint-eyes squared,
tunneled nerves unstrung, you wept with Poe
in a subway dirge where witless faces hung.

Boot-strapped, held tight to a ceiling light

you charged mute fate with an angry plea;
drank tea-leaves from a wino's cup,
a sign you followed to the star-crossed sea.
Aztec glints lay altars bare, ages overrun,
you fed the hungry hound's tooth oath
to trade the eagle for the Sun.

DANCING SCHOOL

"Pick your partners," she cooed to
small boys on one side of the room
ruffling their puberty feathers.
On the other, mired in a gaggle
of girls, I dug in my heels and waited,
a taffeta balloon who should never
have been shod in black patent leather.

White-gloved, my pigtails sacrificed
to a frizzy perm, I braced myself
to withstand the sudden flight
of young boys cruising past me
to circle perfect pre-pubescent girls,
coiffed and forever bright
in their designer plumage.

Peacock proud with natural curls
and Bonwit Teller frocks, I yearned
to learn the secrets they shared
with a flash of an eyelid.
They danced with an ease
I could only calculate,
a grace I would never command.

Scratchy Guy Lombardo signaled
the start of dances my feet refused
to follow in stately fox-trot tempo.
Finally, a leftover wren proffered
me a wing so we could fly against
the walls while the others circled
the room in perfect mating time.

TOTEM

Were her extremities the first to go?
Growing cold while shiny new brain waves
Sent signals to drag me to her shore
Where I could be a final witness.
All I saw were toes curled
Blue with blood wearing thin
And toenails someone had told
Me would grow forever.
From her eyes, she dropped her sex
And from her fingers her grip on mine.

I shall buy a gold fish
And feed it twice a day
So she can swim
Around her bowl
And remember yesterday.

FOR R.D. LAING—TWO KNOTS

Jill knows that Jack can't stand her
yet she follows him up the hill.
Jack knows too as he pushes her down
but again that's half the thrill.

Sally knew that her Mother hated her
but she wouldn't let herself
know that she knew.
Her Mother never knew.
When Sally finally let herself
hate her Mother, her Mother
knew there was something
wrong with Sally.
Sally believed her.

EYEBROW PERFECT

She had had to take three deep breaths
Before she asked, "Do you think I'm pretty?
Her mother was applying lipstick with a brush,
Darkening the outline before blotting her lips
While the sly moon, a Sibyl of lost tides
And changelings watched from outside.

The minute hand reached the ordinal slowly,
As they do in moments when one's pride
Can rise and fall on the weight of a word.
"You have nice eyebrows, they're lush."
She returned to business, smoothing on blush,
Smiling at the hall mirror for one last look.

"Don't forget; turn off the lights when you go to bed."
She left. It mattered little her daughter was bereft.
A sixteen-year-old with too much flesh and eyebrows
To stake your heart on. The moon sighed as tears fell
From a girl first meeting herself in her mother's mirror.
She winced, then smeared an X deep on its face, and wept.

The offending lipstick lay broken on the floor,
Its pieces in Rorschach relief, a portent sign
To her mother, when she opened the door.
It was forgotten however, by a fickle moon
With better things to do tonight than pick up
The pieces to mend another broken heart.

TIWI CHANT

Big Joe, he grew me up.
As promised, he took me,
tasted my tongue
and grew my breasts.
He laid his spear between
my legs to make me murujubara.
He stroked by belly to make
it big with pitapitui.
But no babe.

Big Joe had all his teeth
like the shark.
He had claws like the wild hawk.
But his only brothers
were thief spirits.
All his wives left.
I left too.
He was an empty canoe
without a paddle.

When he dies no one
will dance for him
or climb the fire tree
or carve him a pole.

No one.

LETTER OVERDUE

Daddy, can I send
postcards to the grave?
I was never much of a letter writer
while you murdered sonnets
over a pint of gin.
She won't write but merely
clucks her tongue which never
became her anyway, the bitch.
You should know she's dying now,
ending her days on stiletto heels.
The pounds fly off her,
icy stalactite hard as nails,
as she subways to cobalt
dripping the vital juices
she nailed us with.
Am I getting through, Daddy,
past the calcified lungs,
past the bored attendant
with rake dulled by scraping
leaves from tombed memorials.

Daddy, can I send
postcards to the grave?
You should know your fat zero,
your woman-child still longs to wear
your shoes, tooled and expensive.
I shall walk the normal three paces
behind and cherish my blisters.

My feet will bleed in your footsteps
because you're still wanted, dead or alive.

SUNDAY MORNING

Your half of the bed intrudes on mine
disrupting the flowers on my flannel gown.
I don't want you rooting in my garden,
fondling my breasts to stand up alone,
brash upstarts that will not let me
spread the petals of my dream
or scream if I so choose, or boast

that I'm not dull. I know you are ill.
Haven't I been the deliverer of pills?
the calculator of mercury; pure proof
of your suffering, my husband, my love.
But I still claim the violet coverlet.
I want to follow where life could have led
if I had chosen once to use my head

instead of falling into bed, brood mare
that I am. What's more, most days I don't
give a damn … syrups and unguents are the sap
of my life, living as I do among a forest
of children who grow straight as trees
and smell of pine. But you are feverish today,
a heaviness next to me that weighs down

the branched chorus demanding toast and honey.
Today I wish I had the money to hire a nurse
instead of tending a bore's ear on the pillow next
to mine. I would choose a cruise or shopping
spree where all the gifts were sent to me.
I would will you the boys, jelly-faced and tart
And spend the leftover days mending my heart.

BARN CATS

She knew she would finally leave
the morning he drowned the cats,
a last litter born under the eaves
to the wild calico living off bats,
a wily survivor who freed us of rats.

Shirtless at the sink he stood,
steam rising and falling to stem
their watery reach for breath. Coldly,
he watched them mew black bubbles
transmuting innocence into early death.

It was more than she could bear,
this in-your-face taunt with malice
for all. He had broken his vow
to honor and cherish, turning a pledge
based on joy to a dirge of despair.

Without respite, silence hung heavy
between them, weightier than words,
so much white noise reverberating
across the years, finally spent and
squeezed dry by their mutual fears.

She would take her two children,
the dog, the cat and baby gerbil
without ever once looking back.
She'd follow the road to the highway,
far from kittens tossed aside in a sack.

It was over. She began to pack a bag.
Another for her sons. The sound of water,
still alive and running in the kitchen,
would never turn off the calico howls
of a mother-cat meowing for her young.

PAIN

I learn no lessons from pain.
It offers no glory or grace,
Stamina alone cannot maintain
a body that's lost the race.

Pain is a shroud enclosing you.,
locking you in, a tightening belt.
Pain is prodigious with no rules
to regulate how or when it is felt.

Instead of learning to bear it
And gain kudos for a brave heart,
Pain mocks my steely resolve
to endure the tearing apart.

of a body now lost in itself
far from thought or prayer,
for a body still seeking solace
for pain that's too hard to bear.

HOW MANY YEARS, MOTHER?

How many years, Mother
have been stacked like stairs too hard to climb
since Daddy died at the unseemly age of forty-two?
Too many, when you start counting at thirteen,
an age of tenuous innocence broken only by
rage at Daddy for abandonment on a grand scale.

It was a dire desertion of us both, Mother,
a departure so sudden it dealt a death-blow
to a nuclear family without a relative in sight.
The weather of my world lost its mellow glow
to become a landscape of famine and blight.

If there was fault, it was yours alone to claim.
Where we lived, every cookie had a chocolate chip,
hand-baked by Donna Reed, but you worked
when it wasn't even hip. You also didn't bake
but drank martinis and left nurturing to the maid.

For many years, I used tunnel-vision to secure
memories of life after his untimely demise.
You were forty-three, ancient in my lexicon
of age-related crimes. A sudden widow, you now
performed set duties befitting a paragon of grief.

But I could not define your grief. I did not see
the pounds flying off you or your adolescent bra
as poignant remains of once-in-a-lifetime loss.
I gained no solace from weepy words of promise
falling on ears deaf to the lure of parental hyperbole.

In those years after his death, my teenage years,
you wanted to include me on your list of friends
while I craved some pop image of generic Mom.
I denied and fought you with my every breath
determined to sanctify his life to the very end.

If we had been able to reach across the emptiness
left between us after his departure, we might have
found comfort, a mutual recognition beyond the spite
that ran interference and kept us forever apart,
each trying to forget and mend a broken heart.

ABBREVIATIONS

R.P.M.

How many revolutions rotate per minute?
ripening in clever young clocks
who wear real jewels and swing
their golden wheels with savagery.
Idolatrous, with no respect for time
their stems knock off the minutes
for them with precise perfection
while I must struggle to wind myself
jerking my hands just to keep pace
with their braless ticking.

PAPER DOLL

Paper doll, paper doll
With neat lined edges.
Dress her in gold lame
And she will shine for you,
Offer you a stenciled smile.
But dress her in rags
And she will become a drone,
Drab and lack-luster.
She is just a toy
With a cardboard mind,
A witless blotter
And your best excuse.

FINGERPRINTS

You cannot have my thumbs;
you with your acid tongue
in cheeky cheeks like squirrels.
I'll shake hands anytime
But my fingerprints must remain
Mine alone, unstrung to play
any instrument. I must identify
myself and hang in my own rogues'
gallery of today's most wanted.

CIRCUMFERENCE

I do not want to be a circle
with all my lines neatly meshed;
a Cadmean victory at most
while parallels scour the skies.
Easy enough to stay, I'm sure,
within the confines of womenfolk
but I itch to free myself and soar
above alien currents on alien shores.

I refuse to be squared and put away
like pots and pans in a bottom drawer.

CONVERSION BY LIMITATION

My essence is static;
it's the weights and measures
which must melt ice to blood
for I was packaged early
in the embryonic stage and you
must permit a sympathetic rage
to crack the egg before it spoils.
I do not want to be soft-boiled
or coddled but fertilized
and hatched to possibilities
beyond a crowded coop.
Headless hens bled gently
featherless and soiled,
hold no appeal.

I want to be a pet
with house privileges.

LIES

Lies,
Baby teeth
Sown too deeply
To uproot.
For every one
An even dozen bloom.
Each one perfect.
Each one beautiful.
Each one deadly.
Dozens upon dozens
Of still-born blossoms
Calculating the way
My world will end.

They take my breath away.

TEST

Drink your fill of me.
I have emptied myself for you.
My roots are dry and itching
to loosen their grip on the ground
that shakes in your terrible wind.

If I do not satisfy
will you try a graft?
Just use my eyes. I'll be happy
to become another paste-up job
mannequin foolish without will or way.

AMAGANSETT

Snips and snails,
more cocks than tails,
bay scallops are the best
while toothpick shrimp
and artichoke hearts
wait to stab the rest.
Thermosed martinis vie
with bikinis on bodies
beached and baked bare;
then it's back to soirees
of cocks and tails where
tails wiggle like worms
and cocks like hooks
come in for the kill
and find themselves
out of sperm.

LOSS

Please be gentle.
I am fragile
And afraid to break.
Let your hands use ESP
And follow the curves
That will shape your love
As well as mine.

Softly now.
I am committed
To be opened
Like an egg.

My yolk is yours,
Bloodspot and all.

CONTRACT

In this makeshift world
Of bottom lines
And high tech perks
John Hancock's
Can still be forged.
No contract has yet
Been drawn that
Spells commitment
To a generation
Brought up to plug in,
Sign on and surf
The waves of the Web.

PASSPORT

My stamped identity
Is proof of my endurance.
Don't sneer. It says right there
I'm a person, a female person
with gears greased
to propagate the race.

See that snapshot,
a split-second flash.
I'm as real as the next one.
Prove that I'm not.
Prove that I'm ash.

REPLY

Your words are just wires to me now
and I'm no fearless acrobat.
I'm unbalanced, can hardly tie my shoes
much less hang by my teeth with no
safety net to secure somersaults for you,
the ones that pleased your eyes
and turned your thighs
in my direction so long ago.
Go find yourself an arbitrary gymnast
or a puppet hung up on strings.

As for me, I'm still sorting out
The love-bites from the stings.

POINT OF VIEW

You are both the axis and the pole
While I am merely ecliptic,
Standard and stationary
A zero on the map.
You are both the sense and soul
While I fall in the class
Of nutrients like oranges
To be eaten and thrown away.
My rind may nourish the soil,
Feed and revive the young;
Good fertilizer, better dung.

But I too would like
To revolve around the sun
If only for one day.

I LIVE IN A STAR

Inside a star
Lined with glazed nothing
That creeps down
The black string
Moonward is me.

Cacophony of night
They crash and
To the nowhere
Scatter screaming
To become a something.

And here I live in
And sell opinions
To those who
wander sunless
in the God.

Unable to forge
A separate peace
I choke on isolated death.

NEXT TO YOU

Let me lie
Next to you
And feel safe
In an intimacy
More powerful
Than passion.
Knees bent,
Curved against your back
I hold on to you,
my ballast, my buoy.
I am rocked to sleep
In the ocean of your arms.

Without you
I'm adrift.

RECOVERY

Maybe you read about the day
the dunes prospered.
The waves off Amagansett
rushed in and beat the shore
like German hausfraus.
I showed them my back,
wore seaweed for hair,
held out my broken heart,
once a conch now a mollusk
and tried to freeze the waves
with my breath mid-air.

CREDO

I no longer agonize over
the whys and wherefores
of God and Man
or ponder the sequence
of chickens and eggs.
I leave etiologies
to young Nietzsche's
still grappling for sanity
through dour musings..

As for me, I am
learning to focus
on the small things
that stand out alone ...
the first crocus
after winter snow,
a sudden smile,
small acts of kindness.

GIFT

You have given me moments
Of exquisite joy—let me
Accept them in silence
And not question the source.
It is not necessary to parse
All my waking hours into neat
Diagrams of how, when and where.
Joy cannot be articulated.
It is a gift beyond words.

THE PRINCESS IN THE TOWER

Once upon a time,
ages ago, there was
a fat, middle-aged princess
who raged against time.
Her consort turned a deaf ear
and refused to buy a hearing aid.
He read the Leisure pages
of the New York Times
and bought a power mower.
He purchased silver sunglasses
that hid his roving eyes,
followed young girls' asses
and undid his fly.
Everyday he sank lower.

So the Princess railed some more
at the young princes who wore
their hair long like pages
and turned their stereos
up so high it threatened
to break their eardrums.
When they listened at all
it was to their brigade
of friends and not their mother.
They did not speak her language.
They spoke another,
a new lingo studded
with words like mileage,
bad trips and rock groups

with names like Bad Company
and The Grateful Dead
The only words the Princess
understood were Bad Company
so she wailed some more
and treated herself to catered
morsels that tickled her tongue
and made her remember
days of Champagne, shrimp
and artichoke hearts.
She had temper tantrums
befitting an out-of-date debutante.
She stamped her swollen little feet
in her pointy old ballroom slippers

but nobody noticed
or seemed to care.
She had to shout
or pull her hair out.
She had long forgotten
how to pout and considered
her husband a tasteless lout
who kept leaving his teeth about.
Still no one would listen,
so she fled to the tower bedroom ...
the one with the skylight
and walls of glass overlooking
the unmowed lawn, once the site
of a promised pool now long gone.

It never did hold water.
The tower room boasted a bed
with spools and an orthopedic
mattress fit for princesses
preoccupied with peas.
She read old Alumni magazines
about aging ex-classmates
named Muffy and Moo
who ran Jr. Leagues
and had perpetual tans
to hide all the bruises
of their back-to-back cruises.
through dangerous waters
with uncharted men.

The Princess had married
beneath her although
he had presentable ties,
both black and white,
but he did not appreciate
the blue blood flowing
through her varicose veins
or the pains she took
to erase them so she
jumped up and down
again and shook her fists
at the Chippendale mirror
hung high on the wall,
the one with wavy old glass

that magnified wrinkles
and spotted every rash.
You get the gist.
She hated that mirror
reflecting what a fizz her body—
perm frizz had tangled into.
Once she had boasted hair
that reached her waist
like a braided rope
thick as a seaman's.
Her princelings had swung
on its waves like
a Rapunzel swing long
before they could walk.

Her husband had loosened it
with kisses and caressed
it with a silver brush.
He had buried himself in it.
Now it was scruffy and dank
as the unclipped poodle
no one ever groomed.
Her husband no longer
sunk himself in anything
deeper that the Eames chair
or last month's Playboy.
replete with bunnies.
When he shared the tower room,
which was not often,

he was bored and came too soon
or snored and played buffoon
where once they had made
love 'til high noon, whispered
pillow talk, nibbled ears
and locked the room.
Now the Princess slept alone
shedding precious tears
that fell on her pillow
sharp as diamonds.
The morning sun from
the skylight was bright
as an electron microscope
as she lay exposed

naked on the bed,
like a beetle in a bottle
or a cricket in a jar.
She felt her true self
lived on in a body
that was now a prison.
She was a butterfly
locked in a prism,
a captive Monarch
unable to beat her wings
or flirt with the flowers.
No longer could she sing,
fly high on thermals or dance
to the rites of Spring.

The Princess had a secret
too terrible to share,
too terrible for even her to bear.
Her Mother, the old Queen,
(not being keen on competition)
had mixed with her porridge
a secret potion to keep
her a golden girl-child forever.
It had worked splendidly when
she bounced on Daddy's knee
and served her well
in her courting days
but lately it was
irksome as the Curse.

She was no more forty
than she was two
but no one knew.
It was her secret
and quite a burden.
She was sixteen; she was forty.
It had been so ordained
when she was betrothed
to the aging consort
she now so loathed.
She couldn't cope with
thick ankles and thinning hair
or a balding partner
she couldn't bear.

So she demanded maidenhair
and shut her eyes tight
and held her breath
when they brought her lilies.
Not for her funeral flowers
with their drooping heads
and smell of death
to remind her that
her dreams were left
devouring themselves
like so many snakes
swallowing their tails.
She could flounder
She could flail,

She could scream
and she could wail
but nothing changed a bit.
Not a whit.
Her sons just turned
the Grateful Dead up higher,
more decibels to split her ears
and drown her words
while her husband
hid her car keys
and spent his nights
in the city.
Each wrinkle, each pound
whispered soon, soon ...

a prophecy ... a prophecy..
you'll have to grow up.
How long can cacti bloom
in a rose garden
or you cavort in this room?
You cannot fly and now
it's much to late to die.
The Grateful Dead
grew louder with each sob.
Her husband hired
a French maid, at last got laid
and went to a Swedish masseuse
while the Princess poured abuse
on his failing eardrums.

The days were getting shorter.
One morning she lost
a tooth. No more
under the pillow,
No more waiting
for the tooth fairy
to reward the loss.
No more playing let's pretend.
A prophecy ... soon ... soon ...
you'll have to grow up.
The very thought
made her throw up.
Daylight Saving
foretold the end.

The golden girl-princess
saw no more the real world
through the glass walls
of the tower room.
She bought new ballet slippers,
a bright red wig, and a glass eye,
green to match her own.
As they led her away
she was doing a jig
to the Grateful Dead,
wearing a borrowed tutu
and tapping her feet to a tune
she could now decode
and sing any old time.

978-0-595-45165-4
0-595-45165-9

Printed in the United States
200386BV00005B/115-120/A

9 780595 451654